Charlotte

D.R.I.V.E

TO PEAK PERFORMANCE

ROY ANDREW MCDONALD

Enjoy the read.

MARCIA M
PUBLISHING HOUSE

D.R.I.V.E ™ to Peak Performance
Authored by Roy Andrew McDonald

Copyright © 2020 Roy Andrew McDonald

All rights reserved Roy Andrew McDonald – Coach Forever Ltd Published by Marcia M Spence of Marcia M Publishing House on behalf of the author in West Bromwich West Midlands the United Kingdom
ISBN: 978-1-913905-15-6

There is a catalogue listing of this publication in The British Library
Cover Design Charlene Hemans of Marcia M Publishing House Photography DW Images Edited and Proofread by Lee Dickinson and Tania Charles Pearson
Design Marcia M Publishing House Editorial and Design Team

This book is not intended as an instruction manual and does not give any guarantees that the tasks or methods will be of benefit to everyone. The reader should make their own decision as to whether the information in this book will be of benefit to them.

READER REVIEWS

Robert Broadstock

Retired Special Needs Transport Manager - Caldas Da Rainha, Portugal.

I found Roy to be an engaging writer proof of which is that I read his book in one sitting. I found that chapter three about life and work in the sixties particularly resonated with me as I had similar experiences.

It was a pleasant and informative read and throughout I felt that It would be suited to a two day training course delivered to a class of students in a business environment rather than a self improving read. As this is in essence what Roy does for a living its hardly surprising.

I have nothing negative to say about the book in fact I have read training manuals and other material on self motivation and team building over the years that were dry to the point of being unpalatable, this was very good.

Would I buy this book as a self improvement aid or a training aid to for staff development? Yes I would.

Aurea Reis – Editorial Reviewer at Marcia M Publishing House

The title is perfect for the book as it is Motivational, Insightful, Inspirational, Interactive, and possibly a mind opener for those who haven't come across the techniques discussed. Surely, it will 'Drive' many people to want to do some work on themselves to see the results that they desire to achieve.

Nathan Williams – Start up,self employed caterer Birmingham UK

I enjoyed reading DRIVE by Roy McDonald, I haven't read for some time, I found it informative and I was inspired to move forward with my vision. I particularly liked that it was not too long. The workbook was a good touch, I did the exercises. A very good book.

Praise for D.R.I.V.E to Peak Performance by Teresa Daniels

DRIVE to Peak Performance is a straightforward book, to finally shift you into action towards a goal that has meaning for you. Roy has created a coaching model based on years of business success in the field, combined with his understanding of how the brain works and where real motivation comes from. Most people think they know what to do but can't seem to do it or even more tragically, work really hard, climb a ladder but end up at the top of the wrong ladder, doing a job that has no meaning for them. Roy takes the reader through a step by step process by asking questions, visualisations and exercises which in turn use all three centres of intelligences; the head, heart and gut to create a strategy and a destination which is authentic for you.

ACKNOWLEDGEMENTS

I would like to thank my wife Karen for her support throughout my journey when I started my business. Her attention to detail enabled me to do what I do best, and that is working with people. What do they say: behind every good man is an equally good woman. Thanks also goes out to my daughters Kim and Felicia for their continued encouragement and suggestions after reading this book.

I am truly grateful for what I have, and I appreciate the love from my father who at the age of ninety-eight still worries and expects a call from me to say that I've arrived safely at home. I love you too, Dad, and we all look forward to you receiving your telegram from the queen.

I would also like to thank the Wilsher Group for training me to be an activator to use C-me Profiling, which is one of the best tools to use for understanding people's behaviour.

Thank you to Mark Peters (Balanced Approach) for training me as an NLP Coach, NLP Master Practitioner and Clinical Hypnotherapist.

Thanks to David Wellbelove (D W Images) for the head shot photo.

Thank you to Marcia M Spence, her editors and her team for getting this book published. The comments, feedback and advice along the way have been invaluable.

CONTENTS

INTRODUCTION 1

CHAPTER 1: WHO AM I? 5

CHAPTER 2: WHAT IS YOUR DESTINATION? 17

CHAPTER 3: THE REALITY FROM YOUR PERSPECTIVE 29

CHAPTER 4: WHO OR WHAT INSPIRES YOU? 37

CHAPTER 5: THE POWER OF VISUALISATION 45

CHAPTER 6: EFFECT 57

CHAPTER 7: SO HERE WE ARE 67

ABOUT THE AUTHOR: ROY ANDREW MCDONALD 93

INTRODUCTION

When I embarked on writing this book, I had several ideas on how to structure it and what content should be in it. Should it be a big book, a small book? You get the picture. It's only when you pick up a pen to start writing that you get an idea of what you want your readers to get from the book. Did I say "pen"? I started to write in my gold-leaf book, and soon realised I'd still need to type it up. Fortunately, I switched medium very soon into the process.

When I created DRIVE™, I was working with another company and we were thrashing out ideas about introducing new material for training and coaching people. The initial thought behind it was based on using my experience in the automotive industry. If you're from the automotive industry, you'll probably agree that, compared with other industries, they're slightly behind the times with technology and processes.

What do I mean by that? Well, let's talk about appraisals or performance development plans. Appraisals, setting objectives and performance development plans are practically non-existent unless as a dealer you're part of a large dealer group. I came up with DRIVE™ as a tool for guiding managers on how to set objectives for their staff and coach them on a one-to-one basis. The reality was, the dealer network didn't buy into it in the way I expected, so I started using DRIVE™ for my own clients and with my leadership training programme.

The information in this book is based on my opinions, plus quotes/statements from professional, credible people.

Enjoy the read. Remember to do your own research and practise using DRIVE™ regularly on yourself and with your clients.

If you want to make notes in the book, you will find worksheets where you can record your answers.

CHAPTER 1
WHO AM I?

G ood question. Just another so-called coach that has read thousands of books, only to summarise them into their own words?

Maybe that's true, but I have a unique skill that's been bestowed on me by this wonderful universe. As you read through the chapters you'll soon realise how I use this skill to enhance people's lives.

Up until the age of eleven, I grew up in an environment that was very happy, with four brothers.

On 7 July 1974, the year "Rock Your Baby" by George McCrae was number one in the R&B charts and the best-selling book was *Watership Down* by Richard Adams, my mother died of cancer.

My memory of that day was a knock on the door from a policeman delivering a message to my dad that Mum had passed away. This day had a massive impact on my brothers and me, changing our destination dramatically. One day, I'll detail chapter and verse of how and what we did to overcome the grief but, right now, let's focus on your destination.

Everything we do in life has a beginning, middle and an end. There's always a destination, regardless of the fact that some people just keep on going, like in the famous *Thelma & Louise* film. Tragically, even they had an end.

Those of you who know me will know I'm a fully qualified coach, Neuro Linguistic Programming (NLP) master practitioner, clinical hypnotherapist, mental health first aider/instructor, certified DISC-accredited trainer and a certified C-me Profile trainer, all of which helps me grasp the human psyche. Now, I didn't tell you this to impress you, but to impress upon you that you can change your course and strive to get whatever you want in life, no matter how old you are.

My first introduction to NLP was in 2010. I'd recently returned from a holiday in Spain with my wife and two daughters with a feeling of embarrassment, shame, humiliation and weakness, which had roots in an unpleasant youthful experience. In the second year of my four-year apprenticeship as a mechanical engineer, all the apprentices were sent on an outward-bound course in Wales. Those courses were very similar to the Duke of Edinburgh's Award scheme. It was July 1981; the same year Lady Diana married Prince Charles and became Princess of Wales. We settled down by a lake to rest and removed our backpacks in the sweltering heat. The temperature was around twenty-five degrees, and everyone was jumping into the water to cool off, except me, as I couldn't swim.

"Jump in," they shouted.

"No thanks," I replied.

"Come on, Roy, jump in; you'll love it."

"Nope, I'm good, thanks."

They persisted and persisted, and peer pressure got the better of me. So, I jumped in, right at the very edge, hoping it was shallow enough for me to stand in. Oops, no bottom! When I eventually came back up, floundering in the water, they thought I was messing about. It soon became apparent, however, that I was drowning, and needed to be rescued by my instructor and someone else.

That single, horrific event left me traumatised – until 2010.

In that year, my wife and I, plus two daughters, went on holiday to Fuengirola on the Costa del Sol. During the holiday, someone had the bright idea of going to a water park. Now, not wishing to put a damper on the idea, I went along with it. So, as we walked around, we came across a huge water slide. The girls and my wife wanted to go up. I wasn't entirely enthralled with the idea.

"Let's have a look at them coming down before we go up," I said.

We stood and watched for a short while until I was satisfied the water was shallow enough for me to stand in. Bingo – I saw a man slide down, smash into the water and then walk to the edge of the pool.

So, off we went. Both daughters went down first, followed by my wife, then me. With my heart in my mouth, I set off. I hit the water at speed, doing a somersault at the same time. When I went to stand up, guess what? No bottom.

All the memories of me as a nineteen-year-old in Wales came flooding back. I panicked and floundered in the water and needed rescuing again. I can't remember how much of the holiday was left. All I can tell you is, it wasn't the same from that point on: I was filled with humiliation.

After the holiday and back at work, I was asked by a colleague, "How was your holiday, Roy?"

I explained to him the holiday was good, with the exception of the near- death experience. OK, this might have been a slight exaggeration, but it felt like it to me. I explained in detail what had happened, and my increasing fear of deep water. He listened and simply said, "I know someone that will help you overcome your fear of deep water. His name is Greg and he lives in Wiltshire. He will use NLP to help you overcome your fear of deep water."

He gave me Greg's number and contact details. I hadn't heard of NLP before that day, and decided to do some research on it.

During my one-to-one session with my manager, he asked if I needed additional training and resources to help me complete my objectives. "Well," I said, "I think an NLP course would be beneficial. I'll send you the details and an outline of how this course would benefit me to complete my objectives and improve my performance."

After reviewing my email, my manager agreed, so I signed up for a four-day diploma course. It changed my life forever. I came away from the four-day course truly enlightened and ready to put into practice what I'd learned. The first thing I needed to do was to book some swimming lessons: Tuesday, 7.30 p.m. at a local swimming pool, would be part of my weekly routine. I found it fascinating, and I'm still baffled and mesmerised by the power of NLP and what took place during the four days.

Let me explain what I mean. The trainer ran through a number of tools and techniques to overcome phobias, fears, anxieties, etc. Then he asked if anyone had a phobia they'd like to overcome.

"I have a fear of deep water, mainly because I can't swim," I said.

"What would you like to do?" he asked.

"I'd like to be one of those people on holiday that jumps off a boat and goes snorkelling or swimming in the sea."

He got me to anchor a thought of treading deep water. He got me to relax, by taking deep breaths, then asked me to visualise myself in the water, feeling confident with no fear, while tapping or touching any part of my body. I chose to tap my right knee. I can't remember the words he used or how he ended my session. All I knew was, when I rocked up at my local swimming baths, I told the instructor it was my first lesson and I wanted to go in the deep end. She looked at me incredulously.

"Are you sure?"

"Yes, I am," I said and, with that, she came over to lead me down to the deep end. Before we set off, I tapped my knee three or four times, and away we went. I felt confident enough in my decision to do it, but I'd be lying if I said I didn't have a few butterflies.

What happened next will stay with me forever. We got to the deep end and she asked me if I was OK. I was absolutely fine. She decided that if I felt confident enough, she'd let go of me, so I could hold on to the edge, while she demonstrated how to tread water.

After the demo, it was my turn. For the first time in my life, at the age of forty-seven, I was in deep water without panicking. You see, my problem wasn't a fear of swimming or going in the water: it was about being out of my depth, so I needed to learn how to tread water. How many times have you felt like you were out of your depth in your business or personal life?

After that, I was able to swim in the deep blue sea in Jamaica.

Since then I've studied and trained to be an NLP master practitioner, helping people to use the power within to increase their performance. NLP is a model of human excellence. You can do anything you want to do, when you know how to use the resources in you. Once you understand the principles of NLP and practise them, you'll realise and notice the benefits it will offer you in your business and personal life.

So, how can it help your business? How can it help you in your personal life? It's a process of studying the patterns of the mind, language and strategies used by successful people. It can be applied to many areas of life – relationships, effective communication, mental performance and even sport. Practical uses of NLP in the world of business can lead to a person becoming more motivated, improving work performance and boosting sales, simply by applying NLP techniques and tools.

Some of you will have read the book by John Whitmore called *Coaching for Performance,* which focuses on the GROW model: Goal–Reality–Options–When. DRIVE™ is similar in its construction, and deeper when it comes to tapping into your unconscious mind.

What makes DRIVE™ an effective coaching tool? It focuses your mind on where you want to get to, and ensures you utilise all your resources using destination, reality, inspiration, visualisation and effect as key elements of this model. My belief is that you all have the ability to channel your thoughts to an area in your mind that fuels the fire and ignites you into taking action. Some might argue that they don't need a book or a motivational speaker to boost them and I say to those people that's great. Not everyone is like that, remember we're all different. My objective in writing this book is to open your eyes and clear a path that will enable you to find your destination. I'll break down the constituent parts below with more details and use questions to guide you through the model. It's important to have an open and free mind when you practise using DRIVE™.

"Too many of us are not living our dreams because we are living our fears."

Les Brown

CHAPTER 2
WHAT IS YOUR DESTINATION?

The D in DRIVE™ is for destination and, in this chapter, we're going to focus on the elements and questions that will bring it to life.

When I ask this question, during a training or coaching session, I sometimes get a blank look from the delegates. The main reason is people generally have no idea. We plod along day by day doing the same thing over and over again, with no change or direction, and getting the same results. I'm not going to mention the famous quote by Albert Einstein which was, "The definition of insanity is doing the same thing over and over again and expecting different results." Why? Because too many people use this quote and I want to be different. Oh and just so you know, the original quote comes from novelist Rita Mae Brown. I'm not sure why the quote was attributed to Einstein; did he have more gravitas than Rita Mae Brown? To move forward and get the results you want, you may need to change direction and whatever you do, ensure you have a clear, defined outcome.

So, what is your destination? In the book *The 7 Habits of Highly Effective People* by Stephen R. Covey, habit number two is to begin with the end in mind. This is where we're starting.

Now stop, pause and ask the question again. This time, put your kindle, book or device down, close your eyes, stay really quiet, and wait for the answer.

If you got an answer, great, write it down or type it into your phone calendar with a reminder every day, week or month. If you didn't get an answer, don't worry, I'm sure you'll get one before you finish this book. I don't expect everyone to have an immediate answer. Some people get it straight away; others will be doing something throughout the day or when they wake up first thing in the morning and, boom, the answer appears out of the blue. Write it down straight away, notice how your feel, notice how many images flash in your mind, notice how excited you become. Maybe you'll have butterflies, or just have a big grin on your face when you know your destination.

When I realised what I wanted to do, I woke up about 2.00 a.m. and didn't sleep after that. So many images, so many ideas, flooded my mind. Eventually it was 7.00 a.m. Bright-eyed and bushy-tailed, I couldn't wait to tell my wife.

The first thing I said to her was, "Good morning." The second thing was, "I've made a monumental decision." Her reply was, "Have you?" When I explained to her that I was going to start my own business as a life coach – well, let me tell you – the picture on her face did not match my excitement and exuberance. As a matter of fact, it was the complete opposite. What was I thinking? Surely she would share the same vision, surely she would understand? Why isn't she excited? Why is she questioning me? Why is she putting a damper on my dreams? I sat up half the night pleased with my decision only to have my dreams shattered.

The lesson here is, whenever you get an epiphany or the light bulb comes on and shines a light on your destination, you might want to consider how you share the information with your partner or people around you. Ideas and dreams are in your head; what you see and how you play it out in your mind, does not automatically transfer to someone else. They can't see what you see straight away, they can't feel your passion, they won't feel your excitement, they just don't get it.

I now know that I sprung it on Karen (my wife), expecting her to say, "Wow, brilliant idea, Roy! You'll be absolutely brilliant running your own business, and you'll make loads of money to give us the security and financial freedom we aspire to. The fact that you're giving up the opportunity to have a very well-paid salary won't be a problem."

Hindsight is wonderful thing, isn't it. What I should have done is map out a plan, do some research, and give her a better insight into what I was going to do. Karen's concern wasn't that she didn't believe in me, it was more to do with the unknown. What if it didn't work? How will we survive, how are we going to pay the mortgage, bills, etc? Her pragmatic and logical thinking was all good, but I didn't want to hear it at that time. Suffice to say, I continued with my decision to run my business and now look at me, I'm an author.

Let's use your powers of imagination. I want you to imagine yourself as a log or piece of wood floating downstream, bobbing up and down, swirling, spinning, dipping under water and back up again. Listen to the rippling sound of the water with a gush and a crash as it hits the rocks beneath you. Look ahead downstream, with no end in sight, still floating, drifting without a care in the world. For some of you, this feels lovely: no pressure, worries, work, nothing to think about.

Imagine yourself in your business life, at work or on a personal basis, doing the same thing: continually drifting, floating, out of control with no direction, no clear vision, no outcome. Every day, week, month, and year, a Groundhog Day.

When I was about nine, I wanted to be a doctor. I'm not entirely sure why, but I loved the idea of helping people, and I was fascinated with a stethoscope. I used to daydream about going to see people in their homes with my very own stethoscope. Now I see people and help to heal their minds as a therapist and trainer. Would you say I've fulfilled my dream? Am I on the road to my destination? The answer is yes, and it was only recently in my life that what I wanted to achieve became crystal clear.

One could say that I'd been drifting and floating for fifty-three years before I finally realised what I wanted to do. It was five years ago, on 7 July, the anniversary of my mother's death, that I was made redundant from a very large corporate company. I knew what I wanted to do, and that was to free myself from working for another corporate company, doing the same thing over and over again, adhering to rules and regulations, with a target strapped to my head each month and each year. Let's go back to you floating and drifting, not knowing where you're going or, if you do, you're not sure how to get there. What do you need to do now to take control of your life? How can you change direction and achieve what you want?

Your journey to where you're going starts now, and when you finish this book, you'll be in a much better place than when you started.

In a world of technology, we find ourselves using a multitude of devices to get to where we want to go, apart from the diehard technophobes who continue to use an A to Z map of the UK or indeed any map, depending on what country you live in. Most of us will use satnav, Google Maps, a TomTom, Garmin or Waze as a means to get to our destination. It's simple: type in a postcode or street name and, within seconds, your route will be mapped. OK, so let's do the same with you. Type in your code, asking the question, "What do I want?"

The difficulty here is deciding on what code to use, right?

We all have our own map of the world, as described by Alfred Korzybski, a Polish scholar who devised the phrase "the map is not the territory." Our internal map of reality is unique; however, there will be some overlap, to a degree. As an example, the overlap will be enough for us to understand, connect with and relate to each other and, beyond that, our maps are unique. So, when you type in your destination, your journey and how you get there will be different to someone else. It's our map that enables or limits us as we go forward in life.

The code to use here is the code of silence. Allow your subconscious mind to come up with the answer. Quieten the mind and be astounded by what you can achieve by listening very carefully.

Here are some questions to help you on the road:

1. What do you want, specifically? (destination)
2. What will happen when you reach your destination?
3. What will happen if you don't get there?
4. How do you know it's worth the journey?

5. How will this affect your business, job or personal life?

For those of you who love to speed read and think this is a race, I urge you to slow down and go back to question number two, read it slowly and, if appropriate, read it out loud. This, of course, assumes you know what your destination is. Remember to stop, pause and wait for the answer.

I use DRIVE™ for business coaching, therapy and for my own activities. As a coach and therapist, I always ask the question, "What do you want, specifically?" This means the destination. What I get as an answer, sometimes, is what clients don't want. This information may be useful; however, my job is to focus their mind on a positive outcome they want.

One of my earlier clients came to see me in a depressed state, crying and with no eye contact whatsoever. When I asked what the main reason for seeing me that day was, I got several answers. They included "I can't do it anymore" and "it's too much." Remember, no eye contact whatsoever, crying and with shoulders slumped. It occurred to me that I needed to break or interrupt the state of her mind. So, I called her name; let's say it was Julie.

Julie looked up and I said to her, "What do you want?"

"I want to clean my room so I can sell my house. It's too big for me now."

After further questioning, it transpired Julie was hoarding, and most of it was in one particular room. What I did with Julie will follow later in the book.

"All you need is the plan, a road map, and the courage to press on to your destination."

Earl Nightingale

CHAPTER 3
THE REALITY FROM YOUR PERSPECTIVE

"Reality: noun, the state of things as they actually exist, as opposed to an idealistic or notional idea of them."

When we analyse the true reality of the current situation, in relation to where we want to be, we sometimes leave out or delete information from our minds. At this point, it's important to be brutally honest, with no stones unturned. Evaluating where we are opens our eyes to see the possibilities of what could be. Equally, it may open your eyes to realise that your destination isn't the right choice for you now.

In my mind, being a doctor was where I wanted to be. Realistically, my level of education and the backing from my father – who worked shifts in the mornings, afternoons, and nights in a factory – was non-existent. His sole aim, as it was for a lot of parents in the 1960s, was to put food on the table, pay the mortgage and clothe us. That was it. He didn't have the money to send us to university and, quite frankly, I wasn't smart enough or, more to the point, didn't think I was smart enough. Besides that, what hope did I have, if I couldn't even pass my 11 Plus?

"Get a trade," is all I used to hear from my dad. "Get a trade." So, guess what? I did. I applied for a job as an electrician, only to be told the vacancy had been filled. However, they did offer me a job as a mechanical fitter, which I accepted after speaking with my dad. So, I started my four-year apprenticeship, which was a City & Guilds with the Engineering Industry Training Board, as it was known then. When the training supervisor offered me the job, he said, "You are the first coloured person I've employed, so don't let me down." I'm pretty sure you wouldn't get away with that today.

So, the reality was I wanted to be an electrician, but ended up being a fully qualified mechanical engineer. Thankfully, I didn't embarrass my black community, and I didn't let him down.

Reality has a whole new meaning for a lot of people today. We're faced with countless reality TV shows, which have many of us fixated on the actions and behaviours of the people on them. What do you think keeps people watching them? Do we have an insatiable appetite for spying on people's lives? Is it voyeurism at an acceptable level? The point is, after watching someone pretend to be someone they're not (adapted persona) for a short time, eventually the real person comes out (natural persona). If you want to get a better understanding of people's behaviours, take a look at the work done by Carl Jung, and take the C-me Profiling questionnaire which will take no more than 10 minutes. Look under services on my website or follow this link: **https://www.coachforever.co.uk/services/c-**

me-colour-profiling/ and then use the booking form expressing your interest to receive the questionnaire.

I love C-me Profiling; I use it for all my one-to-one clients and for 80% of people I train. It's different from other profiling tools because it focuses on our behaviour and generates a report which tells you your preferred ways of doing things. The report is real and if you want to understand yourself, develop yourself and understand others better, look no further.

When you document your reality be brutally honest with yourself right from the get-go; make sure you detail exactly what the current situation is.

Before you go to the questions below, think and imagine, right now, about the log or piece of wood floating on the water. I want you to immerse yourself into a deep state of focus and reality, so deep that every thought, every idea flows effortlessly into each other. Empty your mind as if you were bailing water out of a boat, dumping as much information as you can in the water. Watch as the reality of where you are surfaces.

Ask yourself these questions to help you:

1. Where am I in relation to my destination?
2. What resources have I got?
3. What haven't I got?
4. What do I need?
5. What will be the impact on people closest to me?
6. What is the biggest obstacle I'm facing?
7. What am I passionate about?

It's important to structure what you're doing by writing it down or typing it in your calendar so you can refer to it easily. When you commit any action in writing, it makes it more real and tangible and, somehow, it sticks in the unconscious mind.

The year 1982 was an interesting year, the very same year of the Falklands War. I completed my four years' training in mechanical engineering and then was made redundant. "The Iron Lady", Margaret Thatcher, was in power, and we were recovering from the recession of 1980–1981. I applied for several different roles and, on a couple of occasions, was told I was over-qualified. Pull the other one, mate. Unfortunately, all the firms were in a similar situation: cutting back and not taking on anyone. The company I worked for was called Delta Drawn Metals in Erdington, Birmingham, and it was the first time in history that they didn't take on the apprentices after they completed their apprenticeship.

Eventually, through desperation, I picked up a job at Asda in Aston, shelf-filling to get some cash so I could keep paying for my car. What was real to me then was that I didn't have a job, and no one appeared to want me. I needed cash and felt I'd wasted four years of my life. It wasn't a waste of time at all, if anything it was good grounding for me: I learned a huge amount about myself and a greater understanding of people. My temporary job at Asda, I have to say, was very easy and as always I worked hard and did what I was asked to do. It didn't go unnoticed. I was approached by one of the managers who gave me the opportunity to train as a manager.

What's real for you, or what's your reality? Again, I'm going to ask you to go back and think about the questions above. The questions are designed to make you think. That's right. Think deeper, remember to go beneath the surface and if you feel you have exhausted your thoughts, come back to the surface, take a step back and breathe. This is not a race; it's a process that can be done step by step in your time. Many people make the assumption that they are what they are and can be no more. What if you challenged that thought? Think about this question. If you knew that you could be whatever you want to be and was extremely successful, what steps would you have taken in order to get there? This question focuses your mind by assuming you are already there and opens your mind to the possibility.

If you knew all the answers to the above questions, how would they get you closer to your destination? This style of questioning is explained fully in a wonderful book by Nancy Kline, called *Time to Think*.

Let's go back to Julie. Her reality was that she needed to sell her house, but was unable to do so, due to all the hoarding and mess. This manifested into clutter in her mind, which meant she couldn't think straight, had no clarity of mind, was confused, depressed and couldn't see her way out.

As a coach and therapist, I had the ability to clear a path in her mind so she could move forward freely with a clear vision. I like to think of it as freeing her negative thoughts that were held together by glue. So, rather than having a limiting belief leading to a dead end, it frees someone's mind to see and believe they can get past whatever situation they're in, and it's the most satisfying and rewarding thing you can do.

"So how did you release her from the Super Glue?" I hear you ask. I will cover this under the visualisation chapter.

"If you believe it will work out, you'll see opportunities. If you believe it won't, you will see obstacles."

Wayne Dyer

CHAPTER 4
WHO OR WHAT INSPIRES YOU?

"Inspiration: noun, the process of being mentally stimulated to do or feel something, especially to do something creative."

Some people have a natural ability to get on and do what they need to do, and others are envious of their ability to do that.

When you ask who inspires, some people say to me they inspire themselves. Really?! You inspire yourself?

Surely, there must have been someone or something that influenced you to be the person you are now? No, it's all me, they say. That may well be true for a lot of people and, to be honest, when I pose the question to clients or in a training session, some people struggle to think of an answer.

My dad inspires me. As I write this book, he's ninety-seven years old. His ability to deal with adversity and struggles in life is unbelievable. Back in Jamaica, he was married to his first wife for five years, but he eventually lost her to typhoid fever. They never had any children, and it left my dad devastated. Prior to getting married, his first girlfriend produced two boys out of wedlock – naughty boy. When he left Jamaica to travel to England, he didn't just leave his sons; he sent for them to join him in England, which gave them the opportunity to get a trade. It was a couple of years after losing his first wife that he remarried to my mother, Almena. He had three kids with my mother. Sadly, she died of cancer after nineteen years of marriage. As an eleven-year-old, watching my dad – who in my mind was strong in stature, and a strict disciplinarian – break down and cry while eating his dinner, was a real eye-opener. He never really recovered from this loss, and to this day visits and cares for her grave. Dad, I think, needed a companion to love and care for, and he remarried for the final time four years later to Eileen, my stepmother, and in doing so I gained another brother. Guess what? After thirty years together, we lost her to cancer on 26 October 2008.

How many times can you keep losing someone you love, fight on and come out the other side? What an inspiration! His mental strength, his values, his caring and loving nature has kept him going beyond comprehension. If you have a purpose in life or you know your WHY, as described in Simon Sinek's book *Start with Why*, your destination will be clear. My dad has a purpose, and this is to keep living.

In 1968, my baby brother was born. Unfortunately, he's severely handicapped with Down's syndrome. He can't talk, clothe himself, cook for himself or generally look after himself, and he's always been looked after in a care home. Every other weekend since my mother died, my dad has cared for him and, over the last forty-four years, he's only missed a handful of weekends.

Looking after him gives Dad a purpose and the reason to keep on living. What an inspiration! My inspiration!

Inspiration is a feeling of enthusiasm you get from someone or something that gives you new and creative ideas. Can you cultivate inspiration? Yes, you can. Does it come naturally to you? Being inspired is a key ingredient to my DRIVE™ model; it will motivate you, excite you and give you the desire to take action to reach your destination. You may be aware that in the field of NLP or Cognitive Behavioural Therapy it demonstrates that how we think, feel and act will affect our behaviour. When we make a decision to do something differently, like taking action or moving forward, it evokes different feelings.

So, is it important to be inspired to get what you want, to reach your destination?

What do you think? You may already be on your way to achieving everything you want.

On the other hand, you're reading this book, which means you might be looking for some inspiration to propel you forward.

My dad isn't my only inspiration, in fact there's a plethora of people that inspire me. I started writing this book in July 2018, and stopped and picked it up occasionally. I've just read a book by Peter Thomson called *How to Write Your Business Book in 5 Days or Less*. I'm not using all the tips and methods in his book, only because I'd already started writing mine. It has however inspired me to get writing and to finish it, so thank you, Peter.

My wife and daughters are a huge inspiration for me, along with: Tony Robbins, Les Brown, Simon Sinek, Zig Ziglar, Robert Dilts, Wayne Dyer, Louise Hay, Amy Cuddy, Denzel Washington, Barack Obama, Martin Luther King, Desmond Doss, to name but a few.

Desmond Doss was an American pacifist combat medic and, for those of you that saw the film *Hacksaw Ridge*, you'll remember he was a Seventh-Day Adventist Christian who refused to carry a weapon or firearm of any kind. He became the first conscientious objector to be awarded the Medal of Honour. He went beyond the call of duty, stuck to his beliefs, values and principles and was an inspiration for many soldiers. What an inspiration!

These questions may help you:

1. What books or authors inspire you?
2. Who would you like to model?
3. Think of a friend that has inspired you.
4. Think of a teacher or lecturer that inspired you.
5. Are you inspired by a family member?
6. Have you been inspired by someone you worked with?
7. If you needed to consult the wisest person you know, who would it be?

The point is to harness your preferred sources of inspiration every day. Fill your mind with thoughts of being that person, make a note of how you feel. Imagine being that person, see yourself being an inspiration for someone, hear yourself delivering some words of wisdom to a friend, colleague or family member.

Oh, by the way, you may have heard of *The Unicorn Cookbook* by the author Alix Carey, my stepdaughter. What an inspiration!

"Who that inspires has the gift to pass on for others to follow."

Roy A McDonald

CHAPTER 5
THE POWER OF
VISUALISATION

The power of visualisation, *"Visualisation: noun, the representation of an object, situation, or set of information as a chart or other image or the formation of a mental image of something."*

Visualisation has been widely used in sports psychology for at least thirty years to enhance all aspects of performance. What's interesting is hypnotherapists have been using people's imagination since the eighteenth century. Franz Mesmer, a German physician, used hypnosis in the treatment of patients in Vienna and Paris. One of the key ingredients is getting people to visualise the outcome they want while in a trance.

What I'm about to tell you, to my mind, is vital when using the DRIVE™ model. I've certainly had first-hand experience of using the power of visualisation, and I've used it to great effect with my clients and during training sessions.

In an earlier chapter, I recalled Julie who needed to sell her house but couldn't, due to the amount of stuff she had in a bedroom. Being in a situation where she wasn't able to move forward caused her a physical and mental challenge. She lacked energy, suffered with depression and was very anxious about the prospect of clearing and cleaning the clutter.

Having assessed the situation, I decided the only way for her to move forward was to clear the clutter from her mind with Time Line Therapy.

The first thing I needed to do was make her feel relaxed, so I got her to take three deep breaths, slowly releasing each one, and even more slowly on the last one.

I then got her to stand up, and simply asked her to imagine she was standing on an invisible line. I then asked her to point to where she thought the future was and where the past was. The future was directly in front of her, and the past was behind her.

"Great. I am going to transport you into the future to a point where you will have cleaned your room and cleared the clutter. Are you OK with this?"

"Yes," replied Julie.

I asked her to step onto the imaginary line and then said, "In a minute, I am going to ask you to close your eyes and imagine yourself standing in your bedroom. Before I ask you to close your eyes, please point out to me where you see next Thursday, as this is the day by which you will have achieved your goal of cleaning the room."

Julie, without hesitation, pointed to where she thought Thursday was.

"Brilliant," I said. "Now step forward one week to where you think Thursday of next week is and close your eyes. Now take a deep breath in and slowly release, and again please. Now do it again, one more time, releasing your breath slowly, and feel yourself being completely relaxed."

This is the important part, and where the transformation begins. I asked her to describe the colour of the room, the colour of the wall, what the room smelt like, the colour of the curtains, the colour of the bedsheet and, finally, the colour of the carpet. She answered all the questions except the last one. At this point, she paused, and said she couldn't see the colour of the carpet. I realised she was stuck, and quickly asked her to move whatever it was that was covering the carpet and then tell me what colour it was. Again, without hesitation, eyes closed, she used her hands to move whatever was covering the floor.

"It's a reddish, patterned colour," she exclaimed with excitement.

"Brilliant. We are now going to pick up all the stuff and clutter and place it in a bag. Have you got a bag?"

"Yes," she replied. "What colour is the bag?"

"It's a pink bag."

"Fantastic. Let me know when you have finished clearing the clutter from the carpet."

Having cleared the carpet, she went on to clearing the clothes, moving boxes and emptying the room. When she was satisfied with clearing the room, I asked her to open her eyes and step off the time line.

To my surprise, as we took a breather, she kept looking over at the imaginary line, and then said, "Can I go back on the line now?"

At this moment, I knew she'd moved from a state of depression to one of feeling good about what she'd achieved in her mind's eye.

You see, everything we went through was real to her and it felt good, so much so that she was eager to get back on the line. The power of her visualisation was very strong in her mind's eye. I asked her how she felt, and she said, "Energised."

We finished the session by returning to the present time, and then I said, "With this energy, you will go home and continue to clean your room and, the next time we meet, you can tell me the good news."

The following month, Julie came to me, she was completely different, her eyes filled with excitement and energy, and she was bursting to tell me how she'd got on. Her state of depression had vanished.

She was no longer stuck in the glue of depression and anxiety; her room was clean and she had a clear vision of the direction she wanted to go, and is continuing to make progress.

When we use our imagination to take us to a nice place, like an idyllic island with clear blue water, white sand, a temperature of twenty-eight degrees, sipping a cocktail, beer, ice cool water or even fresh coconut water, feeling completely relaxed, happy and content. How do you feel? Now, listen to the waves crashing against the shore and smell the food cooking on a barbecue nearby – it might be red mullet, which my dad describes as a tasty, fine eating fish, or it might be your traditional jerk chicken, with sweetcorn, breadfruit, or even plantain. If you're not salivating, or feeling the heat and quenching your thirst with your drink, you might want to revisit your powers of visualisation. By the way, my island is in the Caribbean, just in case you hadn't noticed.

Hypno-Coaching is great for moving people on to greater things; using coaching techniques with a splash of conversational hypnotherapy works really well. Hypnotherapists use keywords to bypass the conscious mind, which is the gatekeeper. The aim is to communicate with the unconscious mind, to evoke or illicit the right response to get the desired outcome.

Take a moment to get this image in your mind. I want you to think about a time in your life when you felt really happy or proud of yourself. What you'll notice is you can't help smiling at whatever the occasion was. You can't help feeling good. Why? Because it felt good at the time, right? OK, you may find this easier to do with your eyes closed. Read on first and then do it now and, as you begin to think about this occasion over and over again in your mind's eye, make the picture brighter, clearer, and turn up the sound using an imaginary dial. You'll notice how good you feel and realise you have the power in you to change your state of mind by reflecting on these wonderful, positive thoughts. Once you learn how to feed your mind with the correct words and use this exercise as a means to visualise a positive outcome, you'll realise how easy it is to do as you become proficient at locking into these thoughts.

Visualising is one thing. Taking action is the next thing, and this is where coaching comes into it. You may be aware that visualising something to happen doesn't mean it will. We have to take action; we have to be committed to doing something about it.

Taking the first step with anything can be the biggest and most rewarding step. When you continue to move forward, guess what happens? You FEEL GREAT. Incremental steps work with some people, and huge steps works with others. Find what works for you and stick with it, and remember to reward yourself at each milestone. Visualising your outcome every day and putting it into action will get easier. Your vision will become stronger and stronger each day – full of colour, sounds, smells, feelings and, in some cases, you'll taste the success.

The Inner Game of Tennis by Timothy Gallwey is a great book, originally written for tennis players. Tim talks about forming pictures in your mind, quietening the mind and seeing your strokes and imagining what it feels like when you hit a ball. Is this all pie in the sky? Does it really work? Think about this: all the inventions in the world started with a thought, someone's imagination. The Wright brothers asked the question, "What would it be like if we could fly?" We all know what happens next, right? Going to the moon started as a thought, a vision, in someone's mind. The invention of the car and many more things, which some people were convinced would never happen, started with someone painting a picture in their mind visualising their dream. Trust your imagination, believe in your creativity; be the writer, author, editor and publisher of your life.

Another book worth reading is *The Brain That Changes Itself*, by Dr Norman Doidge. It's all about neuroplasticity, and Doidge reveals our brains' remarkable ability to repair themselves through the power of positive thought.

There are countless examples of how people have used the power of visualisation to great effect. For example, a study conducted by Dr. Biasiotto at the University of Chicago, split people into three groups and tested each on how many basketball free throws they could make.

After this, he had the first group practise free throws every day for an hour for thirty days. The second group just visualised themselves making free throws for thirty days in a classroom. The third group did nothing for thirty days.

After thirty days, he tested them again. The third group, as expected, did not improve. The second group improved by twenty-three percent without touching a basketball! The first group improved by twenty-five percent. As you can see, the difference between the two is marginal.

The idea behind visualising is doing it as often as you can until you begin to feel it in your soul and heart.

What happens next is you allow your subconscious mind to make things happen. The reality is you start to create a positive behaviour that matches your desire. You'll find that it attracts people that match your desire, and it will also produce feelings that match your desire. You're making this as real as you can in your mind's eye, giving you the inspiration to take action as you do whatever you need to do to make it happen.

Questions to help you harness the power of visualisation:

1. Where do you see yourself in three years?
2. Where do you see yourself in five years?
3. What do you look like in the future?
4. What does it feel like?
5. If you had everything you ever wanted, how would it look?
6. How would you like to be remembered?

"Whatever the mind can conceive and believe, it can achieve."

Napoleon Hill

CHAPTER 6
EFFECT

"Effect: noun, a change which is a result or consequence of an action or other cause."

B y now, you should have an idea where this is leading. Remember the log floating down the river with no direction? Let's upgrade you to a raft or, better still, as you've persevered in reading this book to this point, we'll give you a boat with oars.

Now you can control the direction you're going in, so you know where you're heading. How much effort you put into rowing is down to you. If you want to get there quickly, you need to row like a Viking warrior going to battle with no fear, fuelled with excitement. The alternative is to row like an explorer, not knowing where you're going, but still fuelled with excitement and, at the same time, trepidation. This of course is not you, because you know where you're going, what you want, and you know that starting with your WHY (Simon Sinek) is important. You know that to begin with the end in mind is important, and is a solid foundation of your destination (Stephen R. Covey).

When I started this book, my destination was to impart my experience and knowledge of helping people, and to introduce DRIVE™ into your lives. DRIVE™ will be used just like the GROW model (John Whitmore), or the SCORE model (Symptoms–Causes–Outcomes–Resources–Effects) for all you NLP users.

The effect of me writing this book, for example, will produce a number of benefits. They are complete satisfaction, achievement and accomplishment.

As you read this, as promised, I'm already writing my second book, which will have a lot more detail about me and my journey to getting here, and how I combine a psychological behaviour system called C-me Profiling with NLP and hypnotherapy to great effect, which I call Hypno-Coaching.

If you're still working out what you'd like to do, or where you'd like to go, think about what you want most out of life. Think about your current situation, decide what you like about it, and what you dislike about it. What can you change that's in your control?

Here are some questions to help you:

1. Think about what it would be like if you had everything you ever wanted.
2. What would you be doing with your success?
3. Who would you be doing it with?
4. Where would you be?

This, of course, is getting you to think past the blockers stopping you reaching your destination. Think about how it will affect you, your family, partner, wife, husband, girlfriend, boyfriend, children, lover, pets, or friends. How will their lives change, and what will they be doing? This is where you start to realise and be aware that, to get where you want to be will have an impact not just on you, but others, and seeing the effect in your mind's eye will give you insight into the positive side of you revelling in your journey. Notice how satisfying it is for you, and look back in time to see the blood, sweat and tears you put into getting here.

How good does it make you feel?

How rich do you feel with enlightenment and gratification?

You've earned it, now enjoy it and bask without guilt or modesty in your achievements. Celebrate your victory and share it with others

This is the effect. This is what I want you to see, feel, touch, smell, or taste, and when you do, please send me an email to say you've done it.

You're not alone when you have these big dreams and ideas, and sometimes we keep them to ourselves out of fear of being ridiculed by our own family and friends. I say, continue to dream big, and allow the ideas to keep floating into your minds. The people who ridicule you don't have your vision, your DRIVE and commitment to succeed. Let them ridicule you, scorn you; all you need to do is smile at them, knowing you'll prove them all wrong. Many people dream or have a vision of where they'd like to be. If it wasn't for these people, the world and where we are with technology wouldn't be what it is.

It was always my intention to publish a quick-read book, but I must confess I have not written this over a weekend. When I started writing this book, we were hugging, kissing and greeting each other. I think it would be remiss of me if I didn't mention our current situation with the COVID-19 pandemic, which started in Wuhan, China, in 2019, and rapidly spread across the world. On 23 March 2020, Prime Minister Boris Johnson announced his version of a "lockdown", with the slogan "Stay at Home, Protect the NHS, Save Lives" which is still ongoing to date.

Like many business owners around this time, I knew where I was going. I had a vision for the year 2020 and could see it developing. Unfortunately, something that was out of our control knocked some businesses for six. This financial year for my business was going to be a record-breaker. But everything stopped. All my classroom-based training ceased and there was zero income. I have to admire the government in offering companies grants, loans, and furloughing employees, costing billions of pounds. Some companies perished, and some are clinging on for dear life.

As the owner of a small business, it's very easy for me to give it all up and become a delivery driver for DPD, or I could cut the grass for the council. It's simple but rewarding, and there's no stress. But, is that me? Did I start the business with a view to giving up at the first hurdle? Successful people understand that to thrive and bounce back requires adjusting or taking a different route. The destination is still firm in their minds; how they get there doesn't matter, providing it's legal and above board, of course. They're going to get there no matter what, and they have an innate skill to think of alternatives or come up with solutions very quickly. They're not frightened of change, of taking risks; they have self-belief and make decisions quickly, followed up with action.

You might be thinking: that's not me, or I wish I was like that. My question to you is, what's stopping you being like that? What if you developed the mindset of a successful person? How would it make you feel?

I'm passionate about what I do. I love it, and my aim is enlightenment for all who either attend my courses or see me on a one-to-one basis. During lockdown, I've been converting my courses to an online version, which is the same for so many of my fellow trainers. You may recall earlier on in the book that I gave you oars to steer in the direction of where you want to go. Well, this is a case in point. COVID-19 meant I needed to change direction, and needed to adapt; I needed to respond to change. My business is totally web-based now. I've used every conceivable online webinar tool and still experiencing new ones. Some people decided that technology and web-based training was not for them and that it wouldn't work. Newsflash: it's here to stay for a while longer so you'd better get used to it.

I'm a great believer in affirmations. I have five that I say to myself every day, admittedly I do get reminded as they are in my calendar for 6.00 p.m. every day. Will affirmations help you to arrive at your destination? What have you got to lose, give it a whirl, and by doing so you'll start to re-program your mind, which means you will take action.

My destination is clear in my mind, and the effect of me achieving my dream will be evident for all to see.

Now it's your turn to do your thing, DRIVE™ yourself to your destination.

"You can't make decisions based on fear and the possibility of what might happen."

Michelle Obama

CHAPTER 7
SO HERE WE ARE

So here we are almost at the end of the book, but before I go, let me remind you why DRIVE™ will and can play a very important part in your life. Is it important to have a goal? Is it important to know what you want in life? Is it important to have an idea of where you are going? What if you didn't have a clue and you kept going on just living and eventually stumbling onto something? Would that be a bad thing? I haven't got all the answers and I certainly won't pretend that I knew exactly what I wanted right from the beginning.

Some coaches and experts in the field of human transformation would suggest that it's important to have a goal, and yes, I agree to some extent. The thing is some people genuinely haven't got any idea of what they want and where they want to go and, quite frankly, don't even care. When you were a child, adults would ask this question: what do you want to do when you grow up? Interesting question, right? Is that a coaching question in disguise?

Does that question allow the child to look ahead to the future and see themselves working in their dream job, for example, I want to be a fire man, I want to be a doctor, I want to be a vet, I want to be a policeman, I want to be a nurse, I want to be a chef, I want to be a footballer or I want to be a gymnast. It would be unusual to get answers like, I want to be a book publisher, I want to be a mind coach, I want to be a factory worker, I want to sell software to the automotive industry, I want to be an administrator, or I want to be a cleaner, and so on.

As you know, our journey in life can take different routes, detours and even go off-piste. It will be governed by things like your health, your partner, the job you end up taking and many other things. You may set off as a child to be a doctor and, with the right support and guidance, that's exactly what you become. To have that clarity and desire from a young age is good, and if your parents ensure that you stay on track and offer their support financially, spiritually and mentally, you're likely to reach your destination.

Not all of us are privileged to have the backing and the support from our parents; not all of us have the financial backing; and finally not all of us are in a position to think beyond our day-to-day survival.

What this book will do is open your eyes to the possibility of doing something different. Remember, we all have the resources within us to do something bigger than what we're currently doing; we all have the ability to dream and dream big; we all have the ability to change direction and fulfil our ambitions.

Having the conviction and desire to do something special, to do something that you're passionate about, to do something that fills you with contentment and satisfaction, in my mind, is your destination. I'd like to think that I have inspired you to take action to be the person you want to be and have the courage to follow your dreams. Whatever path you're on now, and you know the path isn't the right one for you, start to apply DRIVE™, and notice the change.

You'll begin to create new neural pathways, which will break the old habits in the way you think and create new ones. Some of the delegates and clients that I've trained will testify that I get them to develop new neural pathways, and you can do the same too. Think of it as a workout for the brain, your daily exercise. Do you have a family meal and sit at the table in the same place every time? Be very careful how you approach what I'm about to tell you. The next time you have a meal, say to your family that you want to swap seats for a change. Now, you'll get some resistance because it's their seat and they'll use words like "I can't sit anywhere else because of blah blah blah." Well, that's a belief; a belief that if they sit somewhere else their world will collapse, which of course isn't true. If the person has a known mental ill health disorder and has been diagnosed with Asperger's or autism, routine and having the same thing is important to them, so please be considerate and think about your own personal circumstances. If that exercise is too challenging for you, try this one: whenever you sit down to watch the TV, say to your partner or family, "Let's swap seats tonight." Well, if the meal thing didn't start a bun fight, this certainty will raise some eyebrows. We are so accustomed to our habits that anything outside of that is so uncomfortable that we avoid doing it. The reality is if it feels awkward and weird it's good, because at that moment you are creating new neural pathways. We are mapping out a new route, which is great.

Here's another one for you; this will not cause any friction in your house. When you brush your teeth, using the same hand, I want you stop and pause before you put the brush in your mouth. Now start brushing on the opposite side or a different place to what you'd normally do. Again, this will feel weird, bizarre and strange. I asked you to pause for a reason, and it's the pausing that interrupts the pattern or habit. Then the doing, which is brushing on the opposite side, creates a new pathway. You can apply this exercise to almost everything you do as an autopilot, for example, putting your clothes on, putting your shoes on, putting your mascara or make-up on. You will find you always do the same thing every time or start with one side all the time. What I'm getting you to do is to recognise what you do on autopilot, pause and change what you do occasionally. In doing so, we're training the mind to accept change; we're training the mind to create new habits. If you're a smoker and want to stop smoking, we have to interrupt the habit and create a new habit; a good habit that replaces the smoking. This is why you find some smokers say that whenever they quit they gain weight, and yes they do, because they have created a new habit by eating more.

We're creatures of habit, and I've given you an insight into how to start training your mind. When we do this frequently as an exercise, and you ask those important questions that I mentioned at the beginning of this book, you will help to free your mind to give you the answer to "What is your destination?"

Workbook area for
D.R.I.V.E™

D.R.I.V.E

Destination

Reality

Inspiration

Vision

Effect

Destination

What do you want, specifically? (Destination)

What will happen when you reach your destination?

What will happen if you don't get there?

How do you know it's worth the journey?

How will this affect your business, job or personal life?

Reality

Where am I in relation to my destination?

What resources do I have?

What haven't I got?

What do I need?

What will be the impact on people closest to me?

What is the biggest obstacle I am facing?

What am I passionate about?

Inspiration

What books or authors inspire you?

Who would you like to model?

Think of a friend who has inspired you

Think of a teacher or lecturer who
you admire

Are you inspired by a family member?

Have you been inspired by a someone you have worked with?

If you had to consult the wisest person you know,
who would it be?

Vision

Where do you see yourself in three years?

Where do you see yourself in five years?

What do you look like in the future?

What does it feel like?

If you have everything you ever wanted,
how will it look?

How would you like to be remembered?

Workbook area for D.R.I.V.E™

Effect

Think about what it would be like if you had everything
you ever wanted.

What would you be doing with your success?

Who would you be doing it with?

Where would you be?

Think about how your success will affect you and your family?

ABOUT THE AUTHOR
ROY ANDREW MCDONALD

R oy Andrew McDonald, born in Birmingham in the early 1960s, has two biological daughters with one grandson, and two stepdaughters with two more grandchildren: one girl and one boy.

He is a therapist, coach and mental health first aid instructor. As an MHFA England instructor, he is passionate about changing the narrative around mental health by reducing the stigma and normalising it by discussing it openly with people. He has trained many people to become first aiders in different industry sectors, and now he is focused on helping the BAME community who are still slow at coming forward to talk to someone and invariably bypass all help and end up being sectioned under the Mental Health Act.

The question you should be asking is, will DRIVE™ help someone that has a mental ill health? The answer is yes. However, all cases would need to have been assessed by their GP.

Roy is a highly motivated and enthusiastic professional therapist, coach & trainer. He has the ability to quickly build a rapport with people at all levels. This enables him to get right to the heart of any challenge or issue in an affable and amenable way, with a clear and focused intention of eliciting the desired outcome for the organisation or individual. With fresh eyes, Roy has developed a relaxed and effective style of therapy and coaching using metaphors, profiling and other tools as a means to change how people think, respond, communicate, and change their behaviour. He has successfully coached and trained teams, individuals and senior managers, to achieve their goals and objectives. He is passionate about inspiring and motivating people to push themselves to the next level, conquering fears or limiting beliefs. Roy's experience comes from a range of roles as a therapist, trainer, coach, and manager, which makes his style engaging and pragmatic, full of real-world examples and proven techniques.

- Society of NLP (SNLP) – originally formed by Dr Richard Bandler and Dr John Grinder
- Association of NLP (ANLP)
- Clinical Hypnotherapist (General Hypnotherapy Register)
- Accredited C me Profiling Practitioner
- Accredited DISC practitioner
- Master NLP Practitioner (Neuro Linguistic Practitioner)
- Mental Health First Aid Instructor (MHFA England)

According to the **World Health Organization**, good mental health is when you can:

- ✓ cope with the normal **stresses** of life
- ✓ work productively
- ✓ realise your potential
- ✓ contribute to the community

If you have good mental health, you feel good and generally satisfied with life. You may even feel that you belong to a community and are making a contribution to society.

Our aim is to continue to help remove the stigma and normalise the discussions about mental health and provide early intervention.

Under MHFA – England we train people to become mental health first aiders, giving them the confidence to approach someone that needs help.

coach forever
DRIVE to peak performance

Contact Roy Andrew McDonald

www.coachforever.co.uk

www.marciampublishing.com

Printed in Great Britain
by Amazon